For Lara, Tom, Olly and Maddie, with love and hope for humanity – CB

For Osh, Beth, Jack, Huw and Vi with love – SW

For Hugo, with love – AH

Brimming with creative inspiration, how-to projects, and useful information to enrich your everyday life, Quarto Knows is a favourite destination for those pursuing their interests and passions. Visit our site and dig deeper with our books into your area of interest: Quarto Creates, Quarto Cooks, Quarto Homes, Quarto Lives, Quarto Drives, Quarto Explores, Quarto Gifts, or Quarto Kids.

The publishers and authors would like to thank Alice Roberts, Professor of Public Engagement in Science at the University of Birmingham for her invaluable advice and support as a scientific consultant for this book.

Text © 2019 Catherine Barr and Steve Williams.
Illustrations © 2019 Amy Husband.

First published in 2019 by Frances Lincoln Children's Books, an imprint of The Quarto Group.
The Old Brewery, 6 Blundell Street, London N7 9BH, United Kingdom.
T (0)20 7700 6700 F (0)20 7700 8066 www.QuartoKnows.com

ISBN 978-1-78603-265-2

The illustrations were created with mixed media and collage
Set in Gill Sans

Published by Jenny Broom and Rachel Williams
Designed by Nicola Price
Edited by Kate Davies and Claire Grace
Production by Catherine Cragg

Manufactured in Shenzhen, China HH122018

9 8 7 6 5 4 3 2 1

The Story of
PEOPLE

A first book about humankind

Catherine Barr and **Steve Williams**
Illustrated by **Amy Husband**

Frances Lincoln
Children's Books

woolly mammoth

Millions of years ago when dinosaurs ruled the world, a gigantic rock crashed into our planet.
Clouds of dust blocked out the sun and nothing grew.

The dinosaurs and almost all other life on Earth died ... but somehow, little hairy creatures survived. These little mammals made their homes in spaces dinosaurs left behind.

In Africa, apes and monkeys lived amongst the trees. Some apes started to walk on the ground on two legs, exploring open spaces.

66 – 2 million years ago

great apes

little mammals

Homo erectus were a species of two-legged apes in Africa. They had big brains and long legs, which helped them run to explore grasslands for food. They ate meat, dug up tasty roots and learned to use fire and cook.

2 – 0.5 million years ago

Ouch!

These early humans collected plants and hunted animals. They were 'hunter-gatherers', moving around to find their food. Over time, they walked out of Africa into Asia and eventually their descendants reached the icy winds of Europe.

first paintings

Neanderthals

500,000 – 15,000 years ago

Meanwhile, a new species of human appeared in Africa: *Homo sapiens*. These modern humans had rounder heads and bigger brains. They too began to wander beyond Africa.

As they travelled across Asia and Europe, they met other human groups, like Denisovans and the Neanderthals. But over time these and all other types of humans died out. *Homo sapiens* became the only people left and we are all descended from them.

Homo sapiens

The world warmed, ice melted and families began to grow their own food.

In Mexico, people grew maize, and in the Yangtze Valley in China, they planted rice in fertile fields. They built villages and kept animals for meat, milk and skins.

The hunter-gatherers had become farmers.

maize

Moo!

15,000 – 6,000 years ago

Farmers were able to grow more food than they needed. They began to store it and swap it for other things. This made some people rich.

More children were born and survived to become adults. So the number of humans on Earth began to grow.

first villages

first tamed animals

Families settled in river valleys where crops grew well. Villages grew and spread into cities.

Rich people paid others to work. Some made jewellery and tools from a newly discovered mix of metals called bronze. This was the Bronze Age.

6,000 years ago – 1,200 BCE

Cities grew and people lived in crowded spaces. They caught diseases from animals and there were outbreaks of measles, smallpox and tuberculosis. Battles broke out over precious supplies protected by soldiers on horseback.

In the Middle East and Egypt, harvests were recorded with simple marks and pictures. Over time, these marks formed words that became alphabets. Writing spread across the world.

Discovery of a new metal called iron made life easier for farmers. This was the Iron Age.

Iron farming tools and weapons helped the Bantu peoples from West Africa expand across southern Africa. In Mexico, the Olmec Civilization worked with stone but polished iron to make mirrors and jewellery.

In villages and farms as well as busy cities, people made music, with flutes, rattles and harps. They sang songs and told stories about their lives.

1200 – 500 BCE

Roman road

Mayan temple

500 – 1 BCE

Traders made voyages across oceans and land. In Africa, sails fluttered in bustling ports and horse-drawn carts wound along the Silk Road, a trade route connecting Asia with the Middle East and Europe.

In Greece people talked and argued about their world and for the first time, began to make fair decisions about the way they lived.

In Egypt and China, people studied maths. Later these sums helped Roman engineers build straight roads and design sewers. Roman rulers relaxed with poetry and plays while their slaves worked.

Far away in America, Mayan people built cities with large temples and developed their own way of writing with pictures.

Silk Road

1, 2, 3, 4....

In the Middle East, Muslims followed their
religion, Islam. Across the Mediterranean in Europe, the Roman
Empire collapsed. Without law and order, there was chaos and people turned
to a different religion, Christianity, for help and hope.

While most people struggled to survive, some religious leaders and land owners became rich
and trade boomed. Camels loaded with gold dust, cotton and salt plodded across the Sahara
Desert. Paper was invented in China and news spread along the Silk Road to the rest of the
world. Chinese compasses guided ships searching for spices, silver and gold.

1 CE – 1000 CE

Further east in Asia, fierce tribes conquered lands to create the huge Mongol Empire. They destroyed libraries and laboratories bursting with new ideas about science and medicine.

Across the sea a terrible plague called the Black Death spread west from Asia. It killed many millions of people already weak from war and hunger.

But some found a glimmer of hope even in this dark time. Scientists, architects and engineers began to make buildings, art and music that shaped a brighter future.

European explorers sailed in search of a new trade route to the East, but found the Americas instead.

They conquered these lands, killing local people, destroying ancient cities and bringing disease.

America

The Atlantic Ocean

1500 – 1700 CE

Africa

slaves locked and chained

They sailed to Africa to buy slaves to work on their stolen lands. They took them back, chained up in crowded ships. Many died on these horrific journeys.

A terrible triangle of trade began. Guns and brandy were shipped from Britain to Africa in exchange for slaves. The slaves were sent to America to work in harsh conditions. The sugar and rum that slaves produced were sailed to Europe.

Around the world, kings, queens and emperors began to listen to their people. New parliaments formed, with leaders interested in exploring new knowledge and ideas.

scientist

In the Middle East, Islamic teachers conducted exciting experiments in chemistry, maths and astronomy. They inspired others around the world to explore science and nature.

1700 – 1800 CE

telescope

Ooh what's that?

astronomer

Scientists discovered that our world is a tiny blue dot in a vast universe. They worked out that a force called gravity pulls us down to Earth and pulls planets around the sun.

Until now everything was hand-made and goods were moved by animals or sailing boats.

Everything changed when people started burning coal to make steam. Steam was used to power ships, machines, and trains that all filled with people flooding to the city to work in factories.

Countries became rich as the Industrial Revolution spread but many families lived in poverty. A law was passed to end slavery in Europe and America, but battles for human rights were far from over.

steam train

1800 – 1900 CE

As medicine improved, people began to live longer. Americans drilled for oil and energy became cheap and plentiful, fuelling a modern world.

Women demanded the same rights as men, and in some countries they won the vote.

1850 – 1972 CE

But World Wars raged and at the end of the Second World War two devastating nuclear weapons were dropped on Japan, leaving hundreds of thousands of people dead.

After the war, scientists worked out that life is shaped by a chemical called DNA in living cells. People also began to explore the universe and astronauts finally stepped onto the Moon.

palm oil

Burning fossil fuels is changing the climate. Ice caps are melting and extreme weather is causing famine, poverty and conflict.

We farm almost half of all the land on Earth. So there is less and less space for wild animals to roam and for the plants that we depend on to grow. We are just one of millions of other species on Earth – and we cannot survive alone.

Humans have created machines with artificial brains called robots. If used wisely, new technologies can make peoples' lives better, giving us more time to do other things.

Like all species, we use our skills to survive. Deep inside an Arctic mountain there is a room full of boxes of seeds. These precious supplies mean humans should always be able to grow food on Earth.

By sharing, polluting less, respecting wild places and farming alongside wildlife, there is hope for the future. We can all live in harmony with nature on our beautiful blue planet.

Glossary of useful words

Astronaut – a person trained to go into space and study the universe.

Astronomy – the study of the universe and everything that naturally occurs in space.

BCE – a short way of saying Before the Common Era.

Black Death – a deadly plague that killed millions of people in Europe and Asia in the mid-14th Century, shown by dark marks on people's skin.

CE – a short way of saying Common Era.

Climate change – changes in world weather, most recently caused by human activities such as burning fossil fuels.

Civilisation – an advanced, organised way of life, with laws and written language.

Conqueror – a person who takes control of land, a country or foreign people by force.

Descendant – a person who is related to you and lives after you.

DNA – Stands for deoxyribonucleic acid, a material found in living cells which contains information passed on to the next generation.

Empire – a group of countries living under one ruler.

Fossil fuels – natural fuels made from fossilised plants and animals, for example, coal, oil and natural gas.

Human rights – the basic rights that all people should have, such as justice and the freedom to say what you think.

Hunter gatherer – a person whose way of life involves collecting wild plants and hunting wild animals for food.

Industrial Revolution – the period of time when work began to be done more by steam powered machines in factories and the mass production of goods.

Neanderthal – a type of early human who lived 400,000 to 40,000 years ago.

Nuclear weapon – a deadly weapon created by a massive explosion causing widespread devastation, poisoning and death to people and other living things.

Parliament – a group of people who make laws for a country.

Robot – a machine that can perform some of the same tasks as a human being.

Satellite – an object that is sent into space to travel around planets and gather and send back information.

Silk Road – an ancient trade route between China and southern Europe, across Asia.